JABBERING WITH BING BONG

Chapbooks by Kevin Spenst

Surrey Sonnets (Jackpine Press, 2014)
Pray Goodbye (Alfred Gustav Press, 2013)
Retractable (the serif of nottingham, 2013)
What the Frag Meant (100 tetes press, 2013)
Happy Hollow and the Surrey Suite (self-published, 2012)

KEVIN SPENST
jabbering with bing bong

ANVIL PRESS » VANCOUVER

Copyright © 2015 by Kevin Spenst

All rights reserved. No part of this book may be reproduced by any means without the prior written permission of the publisher, with the exception of brief passages in reviews. Any request for photocopying or other reprographic copying of any part of this book must be directed in writing to access: The Canadian Copyright Licensing Agency, One Yonge Street, Suite 800, Toronto, Ontario, Canada, M5E 1E5.

Anvil Press Publishers Inc.
P.O. Box 3008, Main Post Office
Vancouver, B.C. V6B 3X5 CANADA
www.anvilpress.com

Library and Archives Canada Cataloguing in Publication

    Spenst, Kevin, 1971-, author
        Jabbering with bing bong / Kevin Spenst.

    Poems.
    ISBN 978-1-77214-014-9 (pbk.)

        I. Title.

    PS8637.P478J33 2015   C811'.6   C2015-901618-5

Printed and bound in Canada
Cover art & design by Marc Bell (Front and back cover contain details from *Federally Funded Dance Troop/Dog Shit Artist Residency* (2009), courtesy Marc Bell and Adam Baumgold Gallery (NY)

Interior by HeimatHouse
Represented in Canada by the Publishers Group Canada
Distributed by Raincoast Books

The publisher gratefully acknowledges the financial assistance of the Canada Council for the Arts, the Canada Book Fund, and the Province of British Columbia through the B.C. Arts Council and the Book Publishing Tax Credit.

to Margaret and Abe

Frozen, voiceless, a prisoner without sentence, the mind in the dark has no object to reflect on and no object to limit the endless racing of its reflections. In the end, the fear of the darkness is the fear that the darkness will not end.
— Susan Stewart's *Poetry and the Fate of the Senses*

CONTENTS

NONESUCH SURREY

Outskirts of Nowhere   13
Amongst the Chosen (Oh Yeah!)   14
Cold War Reruns   15
Boy, the Way Glen Miller Played   16
Gibberish   17
Jabberwock, B.C.   18
Margaret   19
The Archeology of Engines   20
Testosterone Pinball   21
Come and Knock on My Door   22
KISS Meets the Phantom of the Park   23
Through the Cracked Looking-Glass   24
Struts and Frets   25
Charis Camp   26
Theological Loopholes   27
Doubled Over in Doubt   28
Voice-Over as Prayer   29
Jabberwock with Me   30
Hashish-Assassin in the Night of Long Knives   31
Nintendo 64   32
Jabberwock AD   33
Death Star Trash Compactor   34
Shifting through Small Talk   35
Pray Goodbye   36

DEFENESTRATING WOLF

Stories   39
A Brief History of Lust   41
Faith in Dirt   42
Fenris Wolf's Headache   43

Bad Rehab 44
Normal Polite Speak He Was Not 45

KITCHENER STREET, SASKATCHEWAN & THE WIDE ENVIRONS

The Biology of Belief 49
Disassembly Lines (1819-2012) 50
Ballad in Crazy Quilts 52
The Death of an Old Landlord 54
Doing the Dishes with Matthew Zapruder 57
An Advantage of Keeping an Unclean Kitchen 58
Ballad in Metal for Christmas 59
Inside Jobs 61
Knuckle Mnemonics 62
Expo '86 65
Wonderful Life 67
Black Box 68
Half Past the Witching Hour 69
Jabbering with Bing Bong 70
Kidney Renal Failure 71
Living in the Future 73
Uncle Willy's Buffet, 74
The Ides of January 75
Pray/Goodbye 77
Incompletes 78
Spaces 79
Living on Borderblur 81
From a Hospital Window 82
Doused in Glitter 83

Notes 85
Acknowledgments 87
About the Author 88

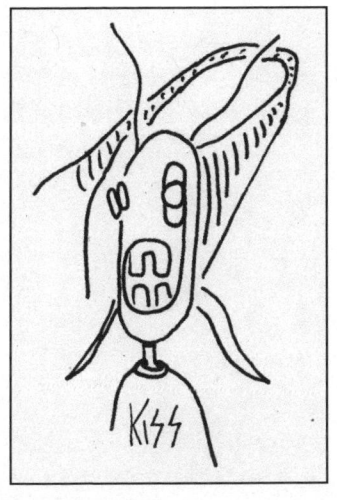

NONESUCH SURREY

OUTSKIRTS OF NOWHERE

From a picture book of canines in tuxedos
waltzing with cats in gowns, I generalized.
Off the page, howls and low hisses were true
to the sidelong conflict between my mom
and dad. I was a blond hairball coughed up
well behind a litter of sisters each scratching
at the door, each dreaming of sound-minded
men who'd bite off no more of the world than
could be chewed. After I found *petting* in an
encyclopedia, I showed it to some gigglers in
the playground. While many were losing parents
or pets to the highway, Judy Bloom and whoever
else we could get our paws on stacked up —
tottering surrogates of frayed binding and spines.

AMONGST THE CHOSEN (OH YEAH!)

We live in Surrey, but we're not of Surrey.
Church lifts us into a different demographic
and summers ascend towards a haven of relatives
in the Interior at OK Falls where we sing in
harmonized prayer: *Praise God from whom all
blessings flow*... best of all you can jump towards
the heavens on the trampoline in bouncing rain.
Better still, I get quarters to go to the corner store
with my cousins. I pick a Hulk comic from the rack.
It goes missing back home: my mom not wanting
anything monstrous to come through the front
door. Kool-Aid crashes through the walls of
news that autumn but we're not in a Jim Jones
jingle. We've been Mennonites for centuries.

COLD WAR RERUNS

Guns are forbidden at home, but I get a pirate's
pistol at Disneyland. The stewardess wraps a white
bag around its handle for the flight. At home
my father sits behind a newspaper: South Korean
Students Riot. Laughter from the sitcom on the TV.
Koreans as polite assistants to American GI's,
cross-dressers and doctors. In the pick-a-stick
trails between houses, guns are abundant. In the living
room we wield the remote like a laser; fire the volume
up for MuchMusic: Scorpions in their cage. My
sister takes me to their concert for my birthday. My
T-shirt of a man with a tattoo gun on a woman's thigh
disappears in the wash. There's no protest. Conflict
has been exiled. Father is so much as microfiche.

BOY, THE WAY GLEN MILLER PLAYED

I believe in Bunker almighty, I also
believe in Meathead his only son-
in-law, married to Gloria who was
conceived of Archie who suffered
under Dingbat, was crucified, dead
and buried under snow when the cable
conked out; he flushed the throne, came
downstairs to watch more from his
favourite chair. Thence he is to judge
the good and bad. I believe in *All in
the Family*, the Holy Tube, the com-
munion of channels and the remission
of reruns, his resurrection in another
series: *Archie Bunker's Place*.

GIBBERISH

is a skill I learned at camp. Our neighbours went
to another kind of church, something more effusive.
One summer I went with Scott to his church's
camp. We were told to open our mouths and speak
as the spirit moved so that the devil wouldn't
understand. I made up sounds, garbled with
belief. Decades later I read from the devil
himself: James Joyce's jigsaw of bluddlefilth, *Finnegans
Wake*, intoned as the spirit moved me through
accents and volumes and felt as if a geyser had opened from
my chest. I got a cheque for my performance.
Confidence powered me through an evening of drinks
with strangers and poets. Sometimes words
mean nothing and everything. Open your mouth and see.

JABBERWOCK, B.C.

The story of Surrey is the history of
traffic. The hysterectomy of engines
is the new direction of suburban planning.
The sublunar landing on native
soil is the corner store of archeology.
The cornerstone of Cloverdale is the
skateboard of literature. The escape
route through litter is the philosophy
of a broken window. The philatelist
of widows is the Taj Mahal of Malls.
The naming of colonial places is the
long division of philology. The looking
glass of Guildford is the resting place
of Charles Dodgson's final subtraction.

MARGARET

He tears up into a creature she doesn't un-
derstand. Her ten-year-old is desperate over
some duckling of a girl. Too young for "un-
requited" but in need of language to soothe
him. No room for a yawn in her open mouth,
even at the end of this glinting day at the K-Mart
jewellery counter where she's had to fend off a schizo-
phrenic husband who hunches in like a spec-
ter around the corner of her lunch break to test
the grounds of the restraining order. Her brothers
were hit upside the head to set up sense inside
but they didn't cry. Whatever she says, she says
slowly waiting for security to come from some-
where as her boy blubbers for a Somebody-Ann.

THE ARCHEOLOGY OF ENGINES

My sister's boyfriend Harold moves his '56
Chevy into the garage. We scour junkyards
for parts, scrub hubcaps in the cement sink in
the basement. We drive to New West to watch
Alien. Harold signs a consent form. The panther
changes from a smiling cartoon to the Restricted
symbol in black. A woman in front of us laughs
when the alien bursts from a belly. My sister
works at Dairy Queen and I think of too many
sundaes. Pain from unpalatable innards will
out. My other sister has a baby. I'm living with
five females. When Gail leaves Harold, she explains
it slowly. He pays my mom to store his car in
the garage. I spray-paint the walls: FUCK. SHIT.

TESTOSTERONE PINBALL

After school, lone boys and boys in packs
groped the iffy edges of a growing habitat.
The Fraser Highway was a river of rubber
and bumpers we kept daring further and further
upstream. The southern forests were sweaty
with bonus points of girlie mags. At Troy's
we pounded a punching bag in his haunted
house of flecked paint. His mom was raising
four kids. His father, the occasional ghost
story. We tried to touch girls at Fleetwood
Park, see them light up — along the path into
the woods where we had the weight to climb
young poplars until they tilted and cracked under
our confusions scrambling upwards to a frenzy.

COME AND KNOCK ON MY DOOR

Our Faller, who art in Santa Monica,
hallowed be thy feigned homosexuality.
Thy cookery come, thy innuendo be
done in a penis stretched to impossible
lengths behind a closed bathroom door.
Give us our blond jokes for a revolving
door of dumb-dumbs and forgive us our
canned laughter as we forgive those who
can their laughter against us and lead us
not into Furley's hammed-up horror mouth,
nor the Ropers' cold matrimonial bed.
For thine is the Jack, the Tripper and
the Ritter, for ever and ever. Credits.

KISS MEETS THE PHANTOM OF THE PARK

While delivering the *Vancouver Sun* after
school, I dream about the new waterslides
at Cultus Lake that coil up like Corvette
mufflers in some animation intro to a film
starring us kids on BMXs, feathered hair
swooshing back like curtains drawing open
our amped-up faces even as our hearts
try to keep it cool as older girls' breasts
brush by our shoulders and waterslides,
like groovy fonts, splash into the next decade
erecting erotic promises formulated deep in
the loins of some lab headed by Dr. Groove-
nstein, a villain from an older decade whose
diabolics collapse. We rock to victory!

THROUGH THE CRACKED LOOKING-GLASS

Johnston Heights Junior Secondary: homeroom
is in Mr. Wright's woodworking class. We sit
in fours on work tables the size of life rafts. Our
feet don't touch the ground. *Do not fool around
or I will hit you*, Mr. Wright says by way of hello.
His black, thick-rimmed glasses give him a Buddy
Holly look, but his bustling muscles make him the
Hulk at his clothes-tearing transformation. *Do not
make me angry!* he says, while we listen to announce-
ments. Chad punches my shoulder repeatedly.
In block F, Mr. Wright. *I'd rather my fist go through
your face, than your hand go through this lathe!* A kid
throws up apropos of nothing and runs to the wash-
room puking on the way. Mr. Wright goes green.

STRUTS AND FRETS

Troy and I are shredding down a hill like
heavy metal guitar solos. Him on a yellow
skateboard; me on a banana seat bike. When
he falls and clamours into a ditch, it's *ka-
pow!* I laugh track myself senseless. Eyes
strung tight, he opens his mouth to spangled
syntax. Cries out from a broken collarbone.
Jed breaks his leg a year later.
      I watch from safety. In grade nine I
grow my hair past my shoulders, get new friends
We break into the abandoned house next door.
Dave spray paints "pussy + cock = fun" in red.
I spray paint a nest of birds black. *You're fuckin'
psycho,* they shout. I open my blue eyes wider.

CHARIS CAMP

is kindness in Greek. Is where Pastor Wally
says *fuck* outside a cabin ransacked for
fun or profit while we blink in the dusk. Is
where troubled kids from Surrey are sent
for last-ditch salvation. Is where we build
bird nests and sing by the campfire: *Give me
gas in my Ford keep me trucking for the Lord.*
Is Capture the Flag divided by a creek we steal
ourselves across at the end of each summer to
race past the off-limits girls' cabins into the
field where the end-of-the-week fire burns
under the Hand of God that shoplifts all the sins
from our hearts. Is weeping for how bad we've
been in the firelight of girls' open mouths.

THEOLOGICAL LOOPHOLES

All my records are thrown into the bonfire.
Every sinner will also burn. Clifford Olson
will gnash his teeth. We sat in the church
he attended. I delivered papers the summer
kids were lured into his vehicle. The blond
boy on the front page of the newspaper who
stopped my aunt's heartbeat for a mistaken
second. How many heartbeats did Olson stop?
In hell he'll writhe next to Hitler and headbangers
unless he begs forgiveness. He could live for
eternity with angels on his lap while the children
he molested wailed below. My Catholic friend
and I debate religion with our History teacher
whose suppositions fall outside a job description.

DOUBLED OVER IN DOUBT

> *By his stripes we are healed.*
> —Stryper

Bible Study on Wednesday. Youth Group
Friday night and then Sunday. At home I
pray over my Bible. A verse suggests going
to pick up garbage from ditches along the Fraser
Highway. The Holy Spirit is a cloud and my
head is the sky. Proof of my faith is in the putting
into action. Someday I will be a pastor with
sermons playing on words for one purpose. Non-
believers are friends in a house on fire. So many
loved ones crushed under blazing damnation.
Come to the concert of God's love! At church
I train as the sound tech: set up stands, levels.
Pastor Wally's mic spikes one Sunday in a piercing
that almost moves people to their knees.

VOICE-OVER AS PRAYER

My three sisters are the Brady girls in
contract negotiations. My mom is the maid
who's taken us away from my father who
is Jim from *Taxi*, scruffily psychotic. He exists
mostly in flashbacks. He drives by to ask
if we need a lift, but we keep walking with friends,
change the subject. Behind the scenes
he suffers the ups and downs of schizophrenia
in New West, Delta, Richmond, moving
between Riverview and any Samaritan of a landlord
who'll take him on. I read the Bible nightly
to find my character, but I'm in none of the begats.
For a season I'm intrigued by *The Wonder
Years*: Kevin narrating his life from some safe future.

JABBERWOCK WITH ME

The biology of belief suspends Darwin's
pants. The suspension of breeches prevents
cruise ships from being hemmed in. The
coordination of colours inside a sound harbour
slips the tongue into the Kinesiology of Suburbia.
The acid reflux of cul-de-sacs informs the
present that the future is warming to the past.
Some Silene-ness in time flowers a colorful gift.
The science of Gifts from Neighbours is an
evolutionary adaptation of arms-length from
an uncertain smile. The phrenology of things
that go David Lynch in the draft beer night
plots a sycamore tree of swings that grow
like branches from the eyes of our childhood.

HASHISH-ASSASSIN IN THE NIGHT OF LONG KNIVES

When my mom's footsteps upstairs slippered off to sleep,
I opened my bedroom window to the Doppler effect
of traffic racing up or down the Fraser Highway.
Kerry took out his father's long-stemmed pipe.
I placed a gold screen in the bowl and then the hash,
lit a match, inhaled and blew smoke out the window.
We took turns until our bodies coughed up a strange state.
Then, we played chess until I found myself impaled
in a brief eternity between a pawn and the Queen.
Time flopped forward like a bad actor's prolonged death.
My dry mouth and stomach chorused hunger.
I crept up the steep, narrow stairs. On all fours, I felt
like an animal climbing out of birth. My red eyes
probed an empty upstairs lit by curtained traffic.

NINTENDO 64

Curtains open, our living room picture window
afforded a view of trees and Coast Meridian crossing
the Fraser Highway. Our TV was the richer land-
scape. One Sunday, after church and hand-
shakes, my sister, her husband and their boys came
over for lunch. I had recorded a game of Super
Mario Brothers onto a videotape. *I
can play with my eyes closed*, I told my nephews; they glared
in disbelief. I pressed play on the VCR, which
was hidden in a cabinet, and then pretended to
eat mushrooms and jump Goombas from memory. At church
their father preached about Christ's miracles, but
here was a feat that secularized wonder.
Charging alongside a maze, eyes closed.

JABBERWOCK AD

The future of Surrey is the Sally-Ann of
Horticulturalism. Charities of Engines
power Deep-Fryers. The Nation-State
of the Unconscious is a Jonah's Wait at
the border. Longboarders will now take
the Theosophists' fast food request. The
keynote speaker at the Golden Dawn
will speak of Lewis Carroll's visitation
rights with certain child actors. High
schools mounting *Alice in Wonderland*
will apply for heritage status for bombing
jokes. Calculus will be cross-referenced with
scripture to begat search engines bringing
Surreyites together in the hardhack afterlife.

DEATH STAR TRASH COMPACTOR

When Luke, Han and Leia shout for joy,
the droids think they're in agony. In grade six
I was dumbfounded by Saudi Arabia. How
many grains of sand? How much past and present?
We learn something; it's barrelled into words,
shipped off. My room in Lumsden has a crack
down one wall. Saskatchewan is shifting. Everyone
is coming for oil. I know about OPEC and the *Star
Wars* marketing of plastic toys. Decades crushed
together. I want to squeeze you in. My new love,
so far away. Your ex-boyfriends compiled into
one rockabilly wannabe with songs about smashing
the rebellion of women who want to be more than
a pin-up on a bicep. You quip like Han. I flutter
like Leia. Is there no Empire we cannot escape?

SHIFTING THROUGH SMALL TALK

I never understood sitting in silence next
to a stranger. Even as a kid on the bus
I wanted to strike up conversation as
easily as a match lights a cigarette.
Inhaled imaginary quips. Exhaled
and choked, tongue-tied on the way
to Guildford Mall or Surrey Place.
I had to wait through twenty years in
a classroom enforcing the friendly rules
of conversation to finally find myself
comfortable inside chit-chat on my
bike to work. To turn to someone at a red
light and talk about her bell, or his panniers
or our sky, our bike paths, our gear in the rain.

PRAY GOODBYE

At sixteen, I folded into prayer for the last back-
and-forth time in my basement bedroom with
one brick wall, and cheap wood siding
and a box-filled fireplace. It was midnight.
The cement floor, covered in carpet scraps,
was equally unseen and cold. The brick wall
stopped halfway, continuing as a ledge of its
lower self, a makeshift closet. An opening at
the end led you under musty clothes toward
a wooden door with a metal latch to a crawl
space under the stairs. A history of fear, of play.
Despite the darkness, my eyes were closed.
I can no longer believe in you, I prayed in bed,
If I'm wrong, I hope I find my way back.

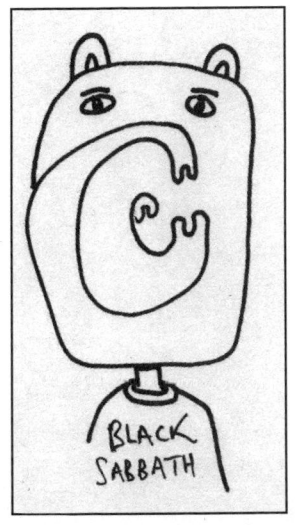

DEFENESTRATING WOLF

STORIES

that are true to life have wolves
in them, says Margaret Atwood. Yes,
once wolves wore party masks

of mice & clowns, frolicked in
make-believe dens with wet bars over-
flowing in martinis and back-

slappery. Wolves extemporized
through belches while their faces slipped
off for stiffer drinks. Plastic cheeks

filled and spirits spilled into the chin
and forehead hollows of their maskbowls.
Hollow eyes dripped gin or whisky.

Libations to everything that goes
down! Doors slam and it's out on the town.
This is neither fairy tale

nor fable. They're swirling
their attention around you and the bars between
just opened under the smashed stars.

Faces sloshed as a toilet swirl. Slasher
flicks tail you along John Carpenter soundtracks.
You thought "once upon" meant "over,"

"at a safe distance," "not eye to eye," "not
the foul red floor of a cave with such big stalactites."
Partially digested etymologists meekly

moaning how "breath" once meant "stink." Now
all you can do is stand some ground. Even pissing
your pants would prove to mark territory. Make
yourself at home. Eventually the belly will be opened.

A BRIEF HISTORY OF LUST

Fenris Wolf Esquire beds Little Red,
colonizes her limbs
in a cherry bowl motel room
rented by the century. Whispers,
is Red your real name? Whispers,
I only feel at home inside you.

FAITH IN DIRT

If the door is a page, it will
wear thin in turning. Bibles
are instruction manuals
for cowardice, thus howls Fenris Wolf.

He casually buries bare-boned
door-to-doorers under the soggy
wash of their parchments.
Fenris clicks his fang with a claw.

Meanwhile downtown, a clearance
sale of crystalline avarice keeps
his wife in a tug-of-war over a chandelier.
She yanks the prize to the checkout
with gemstone snagged fingers.

Later, dinner's served cold outside under
bike frames and Bibles rigged into
falsework against the kitchen window.
Something braised in bacon. Grease

and raindrops drip from plank to plank.
She asks about his day. He answers
swiftly as if gleaning overlooked prey.
At night, they circle each other until

they fall asleep in a swirled ball. In
their dreams they trust each other on special
mendacities for Christmastime or in
the cyanide sweets of All Soul's Eve.

FENRIS WOLF'S HEADACHE

opens like a pomegranate,
stains her dress. Little Red
sentenced to six months hard
listening in the underworld
to his bellyache.

BAD REHAB

Fenris Wolf is treated into the decades
by teams of corkscrew-tailed shrinks
and large-snouted psychiatrists who
grunt like hard rock miners. Penny Duke

Props support a long wall of questions:
*When did you first? When did you first
before that? And how about even before
before?* At the end of tunneled queries, the ground

gives way. The professionals fall through,
landing in a forest of scaffolding holding
up ideas of sunrises, straw bales and squeals.
Broken braces line the brown and red sky.

Here the experts hear words rhythmic
and lost like mapless billowing hills.
The head shrink wipes the sweat off
his brow, wants to throw in the trowel.

He's tired of laying bricks for enclosure,
protection from another blow; he wants
to differentiate, go *wee-wee-wee* all the way home.

NORMAL POLITE SPEAK HE WAS NOT

Some say he was a sheep in wolf's clothing. Even so
he was truly wolf again beneath that cloudy fleece.

He was part hunter, his other half hunting
himself in tales. He played wounded well,

his cry luring moles, voles and rabbits
he genuinely liked. Felt sick to his stomach

picking his teeth with their bones while he studied
analytic playbacks of his dart and chase, kills and misses.

He was a house divided, equally averse to staying
put or leaving. He hoped to be an Everywolf. Everyone's

medieval innards on the rack of conscience and survival.
In any case, when he wasn't an asshole he was real a swell guy.

He'll be missed by some. Occasionally. If you take the bus,
you might think: Oh, he loved racing alongside this thing.

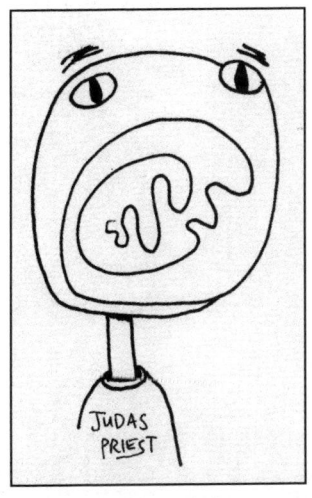

KITCHENER STREET, SASKATCHEWAN & THE WIDE ENVIRONS

THE BIOLOGY OF BELIEF

To imagine God is to invite joy into your heart:
there are no toilets in heaven and therefore no
assholes, intestines, desserts. No cake for a birthday
which is nevertheless celebrated every second on
the second by the firmament of angels. It's happy
birthday to you for eternity and the stars are akin
to the candles for a cake that is the universe — the inverse
of what is felt inside — which is what Michael says in
his speech drowned out by God's yawning. Michael
goes on and on. Everything takes longer in heaven
because everything happens atop everything else.
Nobody cares because they're sharing in a singular
heartbeat and their wildest imaginations glow
from the trinity of mouths and eyes and even the insects
wassail with gobs open wide, filled with the light of liquor.

DISASSEMBLY LINES (1819-2012)

Maybe we ain't got culture, but we're eatin' regular.
                                                —Carl Sandburg

If this song is a factory,
        a hook in the head
                rivets stanch nostrils.

If an open mouth is a factory,
        a bawl bearing spit up
                out of the cradle endlessly—

If Walt Whitman is a factory,
        a beard as a conveyor belt between his gaze and hands
                          a barbaric *yawp, yawp, yawp*.

If pigs are a factory,
            Cincinnati's Deer Creek
                  "Bloody Run" rocking.

If a nursery tale is a factory,
            oinks smashed at the top floor,
                    quartered in a minute by wolves.

If Civil War is a factory,
            squeals sold south to *blam!*
                    Walt dresses screaming wounds.

If anyone is a factory,
            thoughts blank from hands,
                alcohol spills out time.

If Chicago is a factory,
    "Hog butcher for the world."
        Walt's successor's nouns and verbs de-gutted, de-larded.

If appetite is a factory,
        yanked hogs to trolley
            yankie yawps to doodle-dandy
immigrants hum on the killing floor:
        hanging, scalding, cabling, scraping,
            decapitating, splitting, chilling.

If William Klann is a factory,
        surprise of slaughterhouse
            into automotive clang.

If Ford is a factory,
    automobiles as avatars of pigs
        reincarnation in reverse.

If America is a factory,
    freeways as conveyor belts
        cacophony crash and squeal of opinions.

If Ben Hamper is a factory
    Flint Michigan, Greaseball Mecca
        boredom of a Rivethead.

If cheesecake is a factory,
    Walt Whitman Mall
        Song of the Walt Whitman Road, Route 110.

If this unemployed road trip is a factory,
    a tune swerves from a honk,
        a close-call hook in the head.

BALLAD IN CRAZY QUILTS

In the beginning,
the Tree of Knowledge was in
a vending machine. Adam

borrowed two-bits
from that nice Norse fellow
named Buri. The fruit

fell halfway, jammed
behind the glass. Adam
snatched the snake

from under Vishnu's
dream, piped it through
the opening. What-

chamacallits and thing-
amajigs blocked its throat so it could
only fang the fruit. Mean-

while Buri needed
money to buy a thank-you
card for the cow

that had licked him
free from the ginnungagap
ice, so he moseyed

back to Adam's.
The snake was stuck.
Adam asked Eve

to use her little hands
to get in there. *Who's been
tampering with*

my vending machine?
God asked. Adam blamed
everybody, even Vishnu

who just kept snoring
(hence the eviction and a lot of bad
blood between everyone).

THE DEATH OF AN OLD LANDLORD

Reality is a roofless house.
— Susan Steudel

Two wine glasses chime inside
the flimsy cupboards, an annunciated
end to the dishes. I turn from

the draining sink and see nothing
but a tree-green glinted horizon—as if
it's just me, this house and forest.
The phone rings and I answer closer

to the mildewed window which affords
me our East Van back alley view of
rooftop shingles mossy and brown.
It's you. *There are police everywhere.*

Please come outside to meet me. Early
spring blossoms our street beneath
the chestnut trees. Rows of crooked bricks
on end flank our walkway. *Antonio's*

passed, you say, standing at the bottom
step of our cement stoop. Condolences
spring from my throat to the five-o'clock
face of our landlord's son, an unemployed

actor living in the garage. *I broke the door
in because he wasn't answering*, he says. *Now
the police are questioning me.*

Procedure, we reassure him, *standard procedure.*
There's a hole in my heart! he cries. We feel
for his off-kilter grief, but upstairs the smell of
a three-day-old body poltergeists the house,

howls years of awkwardness, the stench of pot
from the couple living in the "garden suite" under the stoop,
where a crack-addict's smoke used to sneak
upstairs into the room of a five-year-old girl

named Freddy—took a year for Antonio
to decide to try to evict him—or the stint
of women living on the main floor who moved
when Antonio groped Jen because she was lesbian

and he was curious, or the afternoon Antonio said
he had mail for you. *Good news?* you joked,
Yes, he replied and handed you an eviction notice
that wrenched you into tears which dried when

I moved in with the agreement to pay more. The first
cheque I gave him: *No bones?* he asked, which you
interpreted as, *I hope it doesn't bounce, kind sir.*
There was always the calendar of naked women in

his hallway above the tacked up headshot of his son
with his shirt off and pants half unbuttoned like some
effigy of fertility. *Ciao,* Landlord. *Ciao.* You will not
stroll Kitchener to Commercial Drive in your suit

and baseball cap, singing the praises of pizza
as an aphrodisiac. In truth, you were more accordion

than harp, more moth than butterfly, more crust
than tomato sauce and salami. *Arrivederci,*

Landlord. *Arrivederci!* all good graces are
temporary real estate. *Inviamo queste parole
con profonda commozione, profondo dolore.*

DOING THE DISHES WITH MATTHEW ZAPRUDER

So much depends on dull moments. I become Matthew Zapruder's 1,458th follower on Twitter and then cross my eyes. The dishes won't do themselves, but an overlapping of the two sinks puts the soaking dishes over the drying ones. Washful thinking. I blink, look up and see a mic over an empty podium. A moment between the introduction and Matthew Zapruder taking the stand. My girlfriend Tawny put up the shelf so we can watch videos on the laptop while doing the dishes. I could address this poem to her. I could say "you" as a thank-you but then where would Zapruder fit in? Late last night, Tawny and I crossed the US-Canadian border. A stream of red lights ahead and white lights on the other side. Podcasts filled the night. The complex eye of the butterfly is made up of hundreds of little eyes. If it sips Rainier beer, will thousands of images overlap? Do you have anything to declare? How is your attention? Strained like eyes from a ten-hour scenic drive along the coast and then a dark freeway? What is your tolerance for name-dropping? I'm also doing dishes with Marc Bell. A Marc Bell T-shirt as a cotton canvas. Marc Bell's a friend of mine. He'd approve of this poem, and he'd be fine with the dishes. He'd draw a facsimile of a stamp of okayness on my dish-washing. I wish I could leave them outside to be washed by the rain, but then where would Matt and Marc be? What if the rain could keep tabs on us? If it were one sentient entity and it saw with every single raindrop? Untold numbers of cars and lanes overlapping. My girlfriend has lost patience by now; she's a fan of comedy or science podcasts. She hates erratic gear changes. On this I-5 who can blame her? The rain watching us from a million different angles like a Marc Bell painting. Zapruder and I talking about Literary Death Matches: my gold in Vancouver and his silver in San Francisco. A Don Domanski line swerves in front of us: *driving this car...this sink full of dishes along the coast.* Our patchwork of social media profiles like soap bubbles on butterfly wings.

AN ADVANTAGE OF KEEPING AN UNCLEAN KITCHEN

A morning ablution in a blink and my contact lens is forgotten. Next, the kettle on the hob, a convex mirror that bends the kitchen into a Parmigianino self-portrait. In this instance, rounded more in grime than renaissance. Some offstage business and the kitchen comes to *me* in the distant odor of dinner from four nights ago. Smoke trellises up from the kettle instead of steam. A noodle from a casserole burns like a slug of incense. The meal we had together between peopled holidays. Our time as if alone but not alone. Two acolytes glommed together in a hold on the uncomfortable couch.

I turn the hood fan on and look again: the noodle, now transfixed in flame. It burns down and steam replaces the smoke. I fill the French press, listen to poetry by John Ashbery and space out over the Christmas tree which is starting to drop questions like candy canes.

There's less than a day left to the year. The changing of the calendars reminds me of my first months in kindergarten. Mrs. Somebody of the giant hooped earrings revealing September: all those empty squares. But a day isn't a square, and a month isn't a rectangle. They're concentric circles in an older model of the universe.

We're the bulbs. Codependent on the bend of a branch.

BALLAD IN METAL FOR CHRISTMAS

From the word go, some
hunted out part-
time jobs at fast food

flop houses to scramble
together enough bones for a good-
bye to some shambling step-

parent who didn't even stand
up for them as classmates in mullets
came to the door for a dust-

up. From the word go, they
shouldered cheap rents
in rooms where toilets over-

flowed, sinks sprayed
their heads off or albums were stolen
in another lock-broken B&E

while they hot-knived
hash under sawed-off two-
liter coolers at some-

body somebody's place.
From the word go, they tra-la-la-ed
over scalpers to concerts

where they lit choruses
with BiC lighters
held high and a lead

singer clenched his
body, screeching as if in transit
straight into a wolf.

From the word
go,
they went caroling.

INSIDE JOBS

Wallace Stevens sold insurance to snowmen. William Carlos Williams doctored notes about plums. bpNichol psychoanalyzed sounds at a commune from the depths of his clients' Ragnarök into scripts for *Fraggle Rock*. Al Purdy built a bridge out of part-time jobs spanning the decades. Bukowski mailmanned all the women. On Leonard Cohen's watch, none of the gangsters, pimps or wrestlers got away.

KNUCKLE MNEMONICS

From chestnut trees a banner hangs,
proclaims in bright pink paint:
Welcome to Kitchener Street!

I'm walking to the bus stop,
thinking about the day that this street
name changed in 1915.

A blond boy walks to Grandview
elementary along Bismarck street. Let's
say his parents are from Germany.

Let's say he's learning English;
he needs help with the months
and their names. Let's say

his teacher, Miss Smith,
asks him to hold up two loose fists,
put his knuckles in a row.

*Big month January,
small month February,* she says
merrily, softly as skin.

The snicker of kids
turns Gerhardt's face red. She
reminds them of their work.

*March is big. It has
thirty-one days but April is small
with thirty.*

On his way home he counts
the snow-coated peaks of
houses white as knuckles,

but at the corner, his street
is gone. Bigger kids block
his path. *Rhinemonkey,* they say.

*Welcome to Kitchener
Street. Your Bismarck stinks
of sauerkraut farts!*

A fist comes down like
a biplane. Later, his mother
soothes; his father

shouts. Or vice
versa. That night he
dreams the sound

of a faucet, but
when he turns
he's standing against

its rushing overflow—
eine mangel of men, uniforms, helmets
mixed in its cold olio.

I see my bus coming
and I hustle to catch it. I need
to get to work on time. I do

have a German in my English class.
He loves Vancouver. Everything is
accessible to him in his wheelchair.

I don't bother bringing
up Bismarck Street. Germans in
Vancouver. *So geht es.*

EXPO '86

The world exposition
was guilty by association. My mom
asked if I wanted to go

with my grandparents
to a preview event. I didn't
know the whoop-di-do

contained the armature
of a riot that would start at a concert
after the singer of

a punk band mooned
the crowd and their sound was
cut. All hell broke

loose. In those days
I watched from a safe distance.
MuchMusic vjs presented

wildness in a warehouse.
That shoot was fucking freezing,
the former bassist of the semi-

notorious Expo
band tells me at a discount
produce store. These days

I know him well enough
to say hi, chat about deals on
red hot peppers or his Chicago

tour with his duo, Canned Ham.
Their public access performance
Who wants a hug? which I sang

for my friends' daughter
for her laughter. The punks have
mellowed. Expo Ernie

auctioned off.
We have not been
the same.

WONDERFUL LIFE

John Berryman, poet, dead man, danced smooth—
shoulders gliding over the floor. You know
that Christmas movie with the prom scene.
The floor opening to a pool. The extras
were nobodies, *coulda bin Berry-men*
tipping closer and closer to the precipice.

His white buckskin shoes kicking up inventive
invective against the Dean. Pal, that
JB could move: glided through
tea dances, coffee hours and coming-
out parties all the way up the Starlight
Roof of the Waldorf. He threw himself

into fun until all was slackened. Mr. Drunk
Mumbles, *I am not, nor have ever been
Henry.* His Booze Angel
showing him the world with his life wiped
off. His Beloved not recognizing him behind
his beard that foxtrotted up as he flew down from the bridge.

BLACK BOX

> *I shout love in a blizzard's*
> *scarf of curling cold*
> —Milton Acorn

The sole evidence of the world outside
is the yellow morning light on the tarps wrapped
around our townhouse. One year ago, they
went up. Now, they are like fields of snow
seen suddenly from the window of a bush
plane turned drink-tippingly to its side,
frozen in an about-to-plummet pose.
The ridges of the tarp suggest a distance where
tundra teems far below with its unseen creatures
and this plane's altimeter spins as we
descend, descend, take until most of the snow melts
before the crashing heat becomes our very own
sun. Bacteria in the digestive tract of a fly
will whisper tales of our calm comportment.

HALF PAST THE WITCHING HOUR

Distant pissing rises in pitch,
fades into the silence of privacy.
We're privy to no other noise
but their Super Bowl brashness.
Through the walls we can see

their faces flush once a year. I'm
nestled in a couch under a slanted
wall, under an incomplete roof and
scaffolding that covers neighbour
after neighbour into the hour of

the wolf. Dreams that terrace down
to what once were mudflats. A tidal
basin that once held up a night sky.
Ursa Major and Minor mirror
themselves, scratch their rumps on

the black remains of the great fire —
bears snoring like nighttime fridges
dreaming a booty of pink salmon.
Pick any point and see yourself to
the door. A mosquito under a paw.

Pigskin splattered a hundred years
ago. A mudflap covered in hundreds
of klicks. Connect the dots in homespun
witchery, soften your eyes and witness
a constellation opening through blue.

JABBERING WITH BING BONG

I worry that our toilet's too small for Tawny's
dreams to come true. For weeks she's been
begging me to pick up a bidet at the hair salon
next to my friends' bookstore. I nose through
the poetry section of The Paper Hound with my eyes
closed, grab a spine, open to a snippet and guess
it's Milton when it's Keats. My ears are in training.
Flush with lyrics swiped from the darkness. Next door
I get my haircut under the tenants of Zoroastrianism:
think good, speak good, do good. This good man
in our country, compliments of the Ayatollah.
Afterwards he takes me to the back closet stacked
to the ceiling. I buy the deluxe model. Tawny jolts
with joy everyday atop our fount of civilization.

KIDNEY RENAL FAILURE

Going upstairs
    is slow. Down,
        he's a reluctant
            slinky.
Little Auggie's
in need of a vet.

Fluids every night.
A needle in back
    of his pinched
        neck.
He hides in our closet;
you cry in full mucus.

Little Auggie's
worn out from brawling
    and balling, from stage—
        diving *à la* Iggy Pop
        into our neighbour's front
        yard concert of flowers.
Fragile as an abandoned nest
when he curls to sleep.

You warn me
you'll collapse
    in a clatter
        of cries
like an old-world widow on a coffin.

At the vet's
his consciousness
   quits with open
        eyes.

He'll no longer
see inside us.

A week later
you weep in
 the kitchen,
  doing
   the dishes.
Hands holding
little things.

LIVING IN THE FUTURE

I first saw some of *2001* in 1983 in Mr. Wallington's
class on a reel-to-reel projector. While
men didn't talk much in the future,
they did communicate to loved
ones on earth via video. It was a long movie
to sit through for us sixth graders. Three warnings

and it was the hall and then sitting on our hands after school,
lot of time to think about the future
and wonder why it wasn't more
like the explosions or even
the cloud city of *Star Wars*. I've time travelled
to 2015, taken the slow route.

At times I talk a lot with men who talk even more.
The future is chattier than Kubrick imagined.
Here in the Qu'Appelle Valley men talk
about hybrid canola, whisky from the town's
drugstore, teenage children, poets, and the pitfalls of nostalgia.
In the evenings, I talk with my girlfriend on my phone. Our smiles

fill the screens in excitement to be holding a version
of one another, but I never imagined this.
I couldn't. The future was a phantom
limb that I felt but knew never
existed, so I return to my mission of eyeballing
the now—that horse in the insect-making distance.

Qu'appelle this? What to call that?

UNCLE WILLY'S BUFFET,

believe it or not, was once the stomping grounds of the only Canadian sumo wrestler who'd thrown in the *mawashi* and come back from Japan having never acclimatized to wiping the derrieres of senior sumos, but instead ended up at Hans and Willy's establishment where they charged him for two and he ate like three sitting as Surrey's very own Mount Fuji in the middle of the restaurant next to Jed and his skater buddies from Cloverdale with their backpacks stuffed with chicken breasts when no one was looking and around the corner from them was the girl with the "what-the-fuck-are-you-looking-at" hair lip and her "well-don't-fuckin'-look-at-me-I-gotta-deal-with-her-all-the-time" boyfriend and then through the swinging doors was the dish-pit drop and then the closet with the two-litre of sweet cooler which we took turns chugging and then through the *thump-thump* doors again, looking at Surrey's Mount Fuji who was in fact smaller than the glass pyramid atop Guildford Mall, but bigger than the cloth I'd used to wipe my first table under the tutelage of Hans who'd just come from East Germany to start a business with Willy who was from West Germany and who liked my Germanic looks enough to forgive my first wipe of crumbs from the table directly onto the floor and next to them was the manager with hair like Roger Daltry who sold coke on the side and my friend Jodi who started a month after me and was always coming down from acid and there I was with my free plate of buffet at the end of the day and all the ice cream I could stomach.

THE IDES OF JANUARY

My job's gone south as international
students migrate home. Now I work
at finding work, dollop the cat his raw
buffalo or kangaroo, try not to let
him escape outside to another scrap.

The chandelier shakes in the middle of things.
The wind yelps through the window.
Outside it's storming cats and dogs territorially.
I must have let him out, I squeak.

In pink crocs covered in paint you
hoot from the front stoop his naaaaaaaaaaaame!

He's pissed with me/   on my rug/
/with the new litter

                /or the fact I'm home everyday.
The cat is the shriveled up head of Archie Bunker
rolling around crankily, making me the freeloading
                               Meathead.

Soon he scampers up the stairs ahead
of you, shiver-shakes himself
in front of your paintings that block
his passage into the living room. Bodies

and faces. A lightning storm of
sinews down a forearm. Braced stolid.
The cat licks himself.

The apparatus of my apology collapses
into kisses from room to room
                to the wilds of distraction.
In bed we agree to let out all the animals.

PRAY/GOODBYE

for Rob

Even under the real mask of bipolar disorder
Halloween is a bad time to kill yourself: an
awkward costume, a shroud of ugly absence.
Earth holds more dead weight. Soggy cardboard
tombstones line the house next door. Anger
lurks behind ghouls at our front door. What we
must offer you is love. You hammered out
the personal into concave dusks, listening spaces
you opened with a tilted head for writing students
and friends. Your ex will go to San Francisco
for eleven days. I wish her warmth. We walk
with heaviness as if gravity has increased.
Saint Suicide, we pray that yours will be
the last. Suspend our disbelief forevermore.

INCOMPLETES

History swells under closed eyes. The December you died. The lacrimal gland in the textbook looked like a giant raincloud over an empty planet. When your eyes were closed, what did you see? An orphan-benefits cheque comes in the mail. In the caves beneath the Zagros mountains some suburban kids warmed themselves with the thought of Childless Profs on the hunt with Adoption Bags. Light flashes through thin skin and becomes what you will. The Gland of Zeis is no myth; it tenures the root of an eyelash. An escaped homebody autopsied across a continent. Solace only in a piss. My semester of Existentialism, Critical Theory, Epistemology, Biology and Chaucer loads a lot onto my mind. Dad, you died at such a distance. The weave of cold water in an inlet comes into a new-found focus. Afloat.

SPACES

The first time I took acid was to understand my father's schizophrenic episodes.

The blotter paper in tinfoil on the tip of my finger like a microchip.

I understood acid in 1988 as a psychotic pick-me-up and breakdown.

Wednesday morning after my mom leaves for work at K-Mart Jodi comes over.

I took acid to get close to a man I was ashamed of being seen with in public.

In the kitchen we open the foil and place blotter paper onto our tongues.

I took acid after reading Albert Hofmann's *LSD: My Problem Child*.

When the cheese in the microwave starts exploding in waves.

I took LSD as a father-and-son heart-to-heart mano-a-mano a mindmeld.

When I step outside the stop sign jumps like a pogo stick.

I took it to be with my father in a straitjacket built for two.

When the sun goes down and someone else's words insinuate themselves into my train of thought like a squall of homeless men in a boxcar huddled in a cold corner.

To travel past his nervous breakdowns in 1954, '55, '58, '59, '71, '78, and '81.

When my insides start to fizzle as if my head has fallen into my stomach I know I don't want to be like my father but no matter how I try I can't shake this tar-thick stickiness spreading.

My father's fear of microchips embedded in medication.

Oozing from breakages inside as we drive around Surrey looking for a place to lay low because we don't dare go home until everyone is fast asleep tucked safely away into their darkness.

LIVING ON BORDERBLUR

Our view of Mount Baker:
a window display of American cake
until a new neighbour is built.

Bugs Bunny steers a motorboat
across the Delaware with Washington.
Foreign cartoons as grandparents.

My father spends long afternoons
seated in the living room as if shag-rug
were looping him down. Sometimes

he's gone and the window is a reality
show of traffic accidents once a month,
flies or other bugs between the panes. In

America, they're crane flies—
in Canada, daddy-long-legs. We grow
up thinking they're leather jackets

(the larvae). Our parents
learned English in kindergarten and slip-
ups are fossilized around the yard.

When I visit a therapist he holds up
shapes, asks questions. Schizophrenia
is a big word for a six-year-old.

I coat my ruler in swirling doodles and
then whiteout which I draw overtop. My gaze
goes down or is drawn to imaginary distances.

FROM A HOSPITAL WINDOW

for John Deakins

The top branches of trees reach barrenly from
green, orange & yellow leaves. Downtown
fails under thick fog. Sunlight stumbles through
to redden brick buildings to the east. We
are less than strangers to billions. Under three
blankets your body seems the thickness of
three blankets. Your breathing rustles into a rasp.
Hodgkin's. When your eyes open, you smile
in the bloom of yesterday's blood transfusion.
At seventy-nine chemotherapy will strip you
down. *To the chagrin of my family, I've been
thinking about death,* you say. We talk books
and the voices that sent Joan of Arc to the stake.
As I leave, your fist rises as a hard-won trophy:
We'll survive ourselves into the vague beyond!

DOUSED IN GLITTER

In the backyard of my heart is a kiln of brick
                               scratched in plot lines
                                       from decades around my birth.

                     My father worked on the Port Mann as a painter
           to take in the grand that went towards their first house.
A chicken in the backyard circling around its head.

The inner kiln is built of firebrick and old Bibles
                               verses against flames against fleshy clay
                                    heated to an immaculate contraption.

                     I was born in the year of George Romero's follow-up
          to *Night of the Living Dead*, a romcom
that flopped. *There's Always Vanilla*.

In-between is filled with flavours of insulation
                               for the pit and firing chambers
                                  the baffles holding lumps of love.

                         My mother was a switchboard operator;
           What if she could have overheard her life
through different circuits?

Would she have demanded a raise?
            Would she have prayed harder?
                      What if she had been Lucille Ball mirroring Harpo?

                     Millions of bacteria reside in our digestive tract;
          play the original mirror scene of Groucho and his double,
but with you and a tower of your bacteria.

What-you-will melts to metaphor to solidify into clarity
        in the dark cliché of the soul.
            MC Hammer or Saint John of the Cross can't touch this.

                We are so attached to our limbs;
    I've got to hand it to your foot;
angels bust moves in the Lucifer Disco.

Ideals are impossible but that doesn't stop us
        from buying calendars with cats dressed
            as the top prophets throughout history.

        A fistula in the side of my head has allowed me
    to poke into my midden of memory
stir my synesthesia widdershins.

The flames of our hearts thumb their noses at our mind
        its limited purview;
           compared to light we are all lopsided.

    Deals are made to be spoken in words that have holes
    in them. As if devilled mice
had nimbled their way inside.

On the clay mug of my heart of hearts let's paint a piña
        colada collage of voices
           sweet and sombre.

NOTES

"Jabberwock, B.C,." "Outskirts of Nowhere," "Boy the Way Glen Miller Played," "Cold War Reruns," "Margaret," "Amongst the Chosen (Oh Yeah!)," "Come and Knock on My Door," "Testosterone Pinball," "The Archeology of Engines," "Through the Cracked Looking Glass," "Voice Over as Prayer," "Struts and Frets," and "Jabberwock A.D." first appeared in earlier forms in the chapbook *Surrey Sonnets* (JackPine Press, 2014)

In "Gibberish" the word *bluddlefilth* is lifted from James Joyce's *Finnegans Wake*.

"Pray Goodbye," "Hashish-Assassin," "Nintendo 64," "The Sally-Ann of Horticulturalism," "Into the Nation-State of the Unconscious," "Fast food for Theosophists," "Shifting through Small Talk," and "The Biology of Belief" first appeared untitled in the chapbook *Pray Goodbye* (The Alfred Gustav Press, 2013).

In Norse mythology, Fenris Wolf is a son of Loki, and is foretold to kill the god Odin during the events of Ragnarök.

"Living in the Future" appeared in *Bare Fiction: Poetry, Fiction, Theater, Review & Comment* (Exeter, UK) July, 2014.

"Ballad in Crazy Quilts" appeared in *Freefall* (Calgary) Winter, 2014.

"Spaces" first appeared in *Poetry Salzburg Review* (Salzburg, Austria) Autumn, 2013.

At John Deakin's memorial service, his extensive library was generously offered to his family and friends. I brought home Whitehead's *Modes of Thought*, where the philosopher writes, "There is always a vague beyond, waiting for penetration in respect to its detail." The last line of "From a Hospital Window" combine's John's last words to me, "We'll survive ourselves" with Whitehead's.

ACKNOWLEDGEMENTS

Gratitude to the UBC Creative Writing Program where Rhea Tregebov, Keith Maillard, Ray Hsu, Elizabeth Ross, Karen Shklanka, Ben Rawluk, and many others encouraged me in my early efforts of writing poetry.

I am forever grateful to everyone at the Sage Hill Writing Retreat for helping me develop many of the poems within *Jabbering with Bing Bong*. Ken Babstock got me started on a sonnet spree and Don McKay brought me Fenris Wolf. Both of their poetics inspired and guided me through the chase for more poems. Invaluable feedback was supplied by my fellow poets: Cassidy McFadzean, Margot Lettner, Ruth Asher, Jacob Scheier, and Brian Campbell, (2012), and Katia Grubisic, Kimmy Beach, Angeline-Schellenberg, Madhur Anand, Henry Rappaport, Kathleen Wall, Heidi Garnett and Dee Hobson-Smith. (2013)

Thank you to David Zieroth of the Alfred Gustav Press and to the collective at JackPine Press for publishing chapbooks which contained earlier incarnations of some of these poems.

A particular thanks to my editor Elizabeth Bachinsky for giving this book such a deft, guiding hand.

Marc Bell is my favourite *Hot Potatoe*.

To my family for their unqualified love and support. To Tawny Blyth Darbyshire for being the love and laughter of my life.

ABOUT THE AUTHOR

In addition to the UK, the United States, Austria and India, Kevin Spenst's poetry has appeared in over a dozen Canadian literary publications. In April and May of 2014 Kevin did a 100-venue reading tour of Canada in support of small poetry presses with his chapbooks *Pray Goodbye* (the Alfred Gustav Press, 2013), *Retractable* (the serif of nottingham, 2013), *Happy Hollow* and the *Surrey Suite* (self-published, 2012), *What the Frag Meant* (100 têtes press, 2014) and *Surrey Sonnets* (JackPine Press, 2014). *Jabbering with Bing Bong* is his first full collection of poetry.